FROM THE MOVIE

Disney · PIXAR

ONWARD

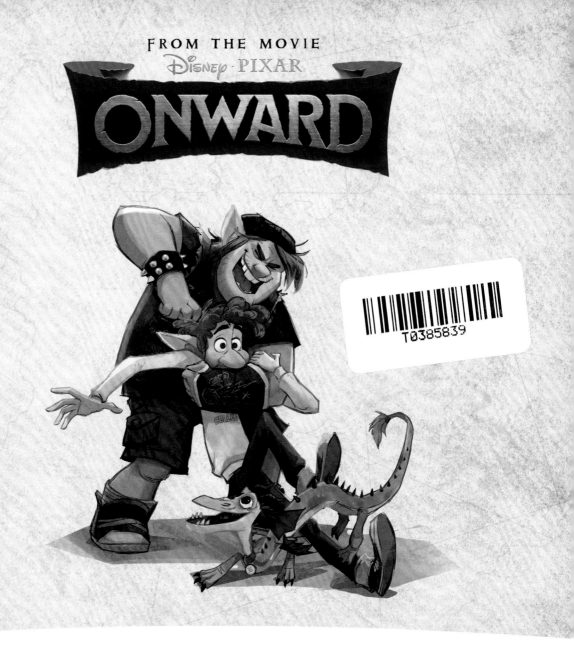

T0385839

Level 6

Re-told by: Lynda Edwards
Series Editor: Rachel Wilson

Contents

In This Book

Ian Lightfoot

A young boy who is shy and scared of everything

Barley Lightfoot

Ian's brother who loves fantasy games and the magic that people used in the past

Laurel Lightfoot

Ian and Barley's mom. She loves her boys and will fight anyone who attacks them.

Wilden Lightfoot

Ian and Barley's dad who died before Ian was born. He was a wizard.

Officer Colt Bronco

Laurel's boyfriend. He is a police officer.

the Manticore (Corey)

Half lion, half dragon, a magical lady who was once fierce and loved adventures

Before You Read

Introduction

Ian Lightfoot lives in a world where adventure and magic have disappeared. Now the people have televisions, lights, and computers, and life is fast and easy. It's Ian's sixteenth birthday. He lives with his mom and brother Barley, but his dad died before he was born. Ian is shy and scared of everything. He is not like his brother Barley, who is scared of nothing. Can a special birthday present bring some magic into Ian's life? Can it help him find the answers to many of his questions? Ian will need to go on a dangerous journey to learn some important lessons.

· ·

Activities

1 **Discuss the questions with a friend.**

1 Who do you think will change the most in the story? Why?

2 Who do you think will be the most interesting? Why?

3 Is it better to be scared of everything, or scared of nothing? Why?

2 **Choose the correct words. You can use the *Glossary*.**

1 The *dragon / wizard* learned to do magic when he was a boy.

2 He went on a *quest / fountain*, it was long and dangerous.

3 He used a *curse / spell* to make a beautiful cake.

4 The king carried a *rope / sword* that was very sharp.

1 Ian Tries New Things

Once the world was full of magic and adventure. It was everywhere. Wizards used magic to help and look after people, but it wasn't easy. New wizards had to learn how to use difficult spells, and many failed.

People found quicker and easier ways to do things. They learned how to light their rooms and build machines. Now televisions, phones, and planes are part of everyone's life and people have forgotten about magic.

Well, most people.

If you know where to look, you can still find some magic in the world. It hasn't disappeared completely …

It was Ian Lightfoot's sixteenth birthday. His mom, Laurel, was planning a party. "You could invite those kids from your science class." She gave him a big hug and his pet dragon jumped on him happily.

"I don't even know them," Ian said shyly.

"Your birthday is when you should try new things, become the new YOU!" Laurel said.

"She's right," Ian thought. He was very different than his brother Barley, his mom, and his dad before he died. They weren't scared of anything. Ian felt like a big baby.

He made some notes.

Today I'll
- be confident
- take a driving lesson
- invite people to my party
- be more like dad

The day didn't go well. First, no one noticed Ian. Then, he got very nervous during his driving lesson. And just as he was inviting some kids to his party, Barley drove up in his old van named Guinevere. *Bang! Bang!*

It was bright blue with a picture of a flying horse on it. Barley was wearing fantasy clothes for Ian's birthday.

"Ha, ha! Is that the birthday boy I see?" Barley loved history and how people spoke in the past.

Ian went very red and said that the party was a mistake. He ran to the van and drove home with his brother.

2 | A Strange Present

At home, Ian crossed off the things on his notes. "I've failed," he thought, and his heart was heavy. "I'll never be confident or popular like Dad." He missed him a lot.

Ian was curious about his dad. "Was Dad always confident?" he asked his mom.

Laurel smiled. "Oh, no!" she said. "It took him a long time to learn who he was." She knew that Ian was feeling sad.

"I have something for you," she said softly. "It's a gift ... from your dad! He said to give you this when you were both over sixteen." She gave the boys a long, thin package.

Excitedly, they opened it. Inside, there was a long piece of wood, a shiny orange stone, and a letter.

"No way!" Barley shouted. "It's a wizard's staff and a Phoenix Gem!"

Ian read the letter. It was a spell so that Dad could visit them. He wanted to see what they were like now.

"This spell brings him back!" Barley's eyes were big and round. "For one whole day, Dad will be back!" They could see Dad, talk to him, and do things together for twenty-four hours.

He put the Phoenix Gem in the end of the staff and read the spell in a loud voice.

Nothing happened. Barley tried again, louder. Nothing. The spell didn't work.

Ian sat alone in his room, sad. The staff was resting on the desk beside him. "What are we doing wrong?" he thought.

He looked at the spell and read it quietly to himself. Suddenly, the Phoenix Gem started to shine, and the staff began to shake.

What? The orange stone was getting brighter and brighter, and something strange was happening in the room. Ian watched as clothes and books rose into the air.

The staff was shaking badly now, and Ian caught it just before it
fell on the floor. When his hands closed around the wood, it shone
with lines of blue light.

"... one day to walk the earth!" Ian completed the spell, and a
great wind came into the room. The books moved quickly in circles
around him. Ian could feel the wind against his face and in his hair.
It was pulling the staff, too. Waves of bright red light shone from
the Phoenix Gem.

Barley ran in. "What are you doing in here?"

"I don't know!" Ian cried as he fought to hold the staff.

Suddenly, fierce, blue light shot from the staff to the floor. Blue stars rained down and started to make a shape.

"Whoa! Feet!" Barley pointed at a pair of shoes. The blue light continued to burn, and above the feet came socks. Then legs. Then a shirt. Then … Suddenly, the blue fire changed to red, and the Phoenix Gem flew off the staff.

The strong wind was pushing Ian back. Barley tried to help him but … *Crash!* The Phoenix Gem broke into pieces, the red fire disappeared, and the magic died.

Dad was gone, and the boys were alone.

3 The Quest Begins

A noise came from the open cupboard. Something was moving under the clothes. Then, the "something" stood up. The boys's mouths fell open. They saw a pair of shoes, socks, and legs, and then … nothing. Soft, blue light shone up from the belt.

"Ah! He's just legs!" Barley cried. The legs moved across the floor and knocked into a desk.

Barley remembered a game with his dad. He tapped his fingers on one of the shoes. The foot tapped back! Then, it touched Ian's foot and Ian softly put his hand on the shoe. Dad was here with them! Well, half of him.

"My little brother has the magic gift!" Barley cried. "But we have to find another Phoenix Gem." He had an idea. In a box of game cards, he found a picture of an old house and another of a fierce creature called a manticore. "We'll start at the place where all quests begin—the Manticore's Tavern!"

"Barley, this is for one of the games," Ian said. But Barley explained that the game got its ideas from real life. He loved everything about magic and the past.

"I'm gonna meet my dad!" Ian said happily.

Barley hugged him. "You hear that, Dad? We're going on a quest!"

In the van, Ian found some old clothes. He used them to make a head, chest, and arms to put on Dad's legs. Now he looked better! Then, Ian wrote notes of things he wanted to do with Dad: *play catch*, *talk about my life*, *laugh together*, *learn to drive* ...

Barley gave Ian a spell book from the game cards. "You're gonna have to practice your magic!"

Ian tried a spell to make things rise. "Aloft Elevar!" he cried, but nothing rose.

"You have to speak from your heart's fire!" Barley told him. Ian tried again but he couldn't do it. And they only had twenty-four hours.

The Manticore Returns

Laurel saw Ian's messy room and the game cards on the table. "Oh, no!" she thought. "What are they doing?" She got in her car and followed the boys to the Manticore's Tavern.

The tavern was mysterious and dark against the night sky. Ian led Dad by a rope and the three went inside. Ian was scared but he got a big surprise.

The place wasn't cold and empty, it was a noisy, family restaurant! People were eating, having parties, and playing games.

The Manticore was carrying plates of food. She was now called Corey, and she wasn't fierce at all!

"Great Manticore!" Barley said loudly. "My brother and I are looking for a map … to a Phoenix Gem."

Corey smiled and gave them a children's menu with pictures to color. Barley saw her old adventure map on the wall and pulled it off, but she took it back.

"My days of sending people on dangerous quests are over," she said, and turned away.

Ian pointed at a picture of the old, fierce Manticore. "Look at that Manticore," he shouted.

Corey looked at the old picture with new eyes. She suddenly realized how different she was now.

"What have I become?" she cried. "Once, I was dangerous and wild!"

It was time to change. Corey opened her wings and breathed fire. Soon, the whole tavern was burning; the map, too! Ian's heart was going fast as they ran to the van.

The map was gone, but they still had the children's menu. On it there was the name of a mountain, "Raven's Point", under a picture of the Phoenix Gem.

Barley wanted to take an old road, the Path of Peril, but Ian thought the expressway was faster. Finally, Barley agreed. *Whoosh!* They joined the traffic. The quest was beginning.

"Oh, no!" Laurel thought when she saw the fire at the Manticore's tavern. There were police officers and hospital vans everywhere. "I'm looking for my two sons!" she shouted.

The Manticore was sitting on the road with a cup of coffee. "They went on a quest to find a Phoenix Gem," she smiled. "Don't worry! I told them about the map, and about the curse."

"The what?" Laurel cried.

"Oh! I forgot the curse!" The Manticore stood up quickly. "But I know where they are going. We can still save them!" They ran to Laurel's car and it raced onto the expressway.

Guinevere coughed and then stopped. No gas. Barley found a plastic bottle in the back, but there was only a little gas in it.

"Is there a magic way to get gas?" Ian asked.

Barley told him a spell to grow things, but it was hard. Ian should only think about the spell—nothing else—or it might go wrong.

"Okay, Magnora Gantuan!" Blue fire shot from the staff again, and the bottle grew bigger. But, as always, Barley couldn't stop talking. Ian looked at him, and the magic stopped. The bottle was small again, but worse—Barley was even smaller! He was like a little doll.

5 Friends and Enemies

Ian put Barley in his shirt pocket and went to look for a gas station. It was a long walk, but they found one.

While Ian was paying for the gas and some snacks, a group of Pixie Dusters arrived on big, fast motorbikes. They climbed all over the station store shelves like angry little insects.

Outside the station store, Dad knocked over all the motorbikes. *CRASH!* "You're dead!" The Dusters cried. They started up their bikes loudly.

Barley was too small to drive. Ian's heart almost stopped. "No, no, no ..." he thought. But he had to be brave. He started the van.

The Dusters were close behind them as they raced toward the expressway. Ian closed his eyes and joined the fast cars. He opened his eyes. Amazing! They were still alive!

The motorbikes tried to push Guinevere off the road. Suddenly, Ian saw the road to the mountains. He drove quickly across the traffic and left the expressway, but the Dusters were going too fast. *Crash!* They screamed as their bikes hit the road.

The Dusters were gone, but Ian had another problem. Little Barley—on Ian's knees—suddenly grew bigger. Ian drove wildly across the road.

Then they heard a police car.

Ian stopped suddenly and Dad fell out of the van. The officer looked at the strange person with no top half.

Barley told Ian to use a disguise spell and only say things that were true. Ian disguised himself as Officer Colt Bronco, Mom's new boyfriend. It worked!

Then the officer started to talk about Barley. She said that he couldn't do anything right and failed at everything. Ian didn't want to agree. Barley was listening! "Um … I don't …". Before he could say "agree", part of the disguise disappeared!

Now Barley knew Ian's real opinion of him.

Back in the van, Barley refused to talk to Ian and turned the music up loud.

Then, they stopped to get some drinks, and something strange happened. The music was still playing in the van and Dad's legs started dancing. He could feel the music in the ground! It was very funny, and Barley started to dance with him. Ian joined them. It was silly, and soon the boys were laughing together.

Barley looked at his young brother. He wanted to do something right. "Just do one thing my way," he said quietly. He really thought the Path of Peril was the best road.

Ian understood what Barley needed to do. "Okay," he said.

The Manticore told Laurel about the curse. If anyone takes the Phoenix Gem, a fierce dragon will rise and attack them. The boys were in danger. But it was okay, because the Manticore could kill the dragon with her magical sword: the Curse Crusher.

There was only one problem. She sold the sword.

The Manticore and Laurel drove to the shop to buy back the Curse Crusher. But the owner realized the sword was important and she asked a high price. So, the Manticore hit her with her tail and she and Laurel escaped with the Curse Crusher.

Then Laurel got a call from Officer Colt Bronco. He was following the boys north.

6 Follow the Birds

Barley drove happily through the night. Now he was in the world of his fantasy game. The Path of Peril was an old road with a lot of holes, and the van threw Ian and Dad from one side to the other.

Suddenly, he heard Ian's voice. "Whoa! Stop!" *SCREECH!* The boys nearly went through the glass.

The road was gone, the land was gone. In front of Guinevere's wheels was a deep, dark valley. They couldn't see the bottom.

Then, Ian looked across the valley. There was an old bridge with a machine to bring it up or drop it. Now it was up.

Barley had a spell to make another bridge, but it was a bridge that no one could see.

"Bridgrigar Invisia!" Ian cried. The staff shone blue, but there was no bridge.

"If you believe the bridge is there, then it's there," Barley said. With a rope around him, Ian put a foot into the air ... and fell down!

He was very scared, but he needed to be brave. "It is there," he thought, and he tried again. This time, Ian's feet touched magical blue stones! Yes!

Ian crossed the empty space and used the machine. The bridge came down.

Above the bridge, there was a big, stone bird. Barley had an idea about the words "Raven's Point" on the menu. Ravens were black birds.

"Maybe it means 'Follow where the bird is pointing!'" he said. They looked and there, over the field, was another stone bird.

A police car drove across the bridge. "You guys are in big trouble!" Officer Colt Bronco said. He ordered the boys to go home.

"Okay." Ian said sadly, then got into the van—and drove off quickly!

Suddenly, behind them they heard not one, but a lot of police cars. Guinevere went faster and faster, until ... the mountain road ended in rocks!

What could they do to stop the police?

Ian tried a spell, but it failed. Then, with a heavy heart, Barley pointed Guinevere toward the police. He started his wonderful van for the last time and stood back.

Alone, Guinevere drove along the road. She hit a rock, flew up into the air and knocked against the side of the mountain. Rocks— and Guinevere—dropped onto the road. *CRASH!* The police cars had to stop. Barley's plan worked.

Now they could follow the stone birds. But the sun was high in the sky. Ian knew that Dad's one day with them was getting shorter.

7 Into the Mountain

The last stone bird was looking down at a metal circle on the ground. It was like a mirror and it showed a point on the bird's body. Ian tapped the point and a stone came out. There was a mysterious picture of a cross and some lines that looked like waves of water.

They looked around and saw a small river that went inside the mountain. They followed it.

Barley pointed to the cross on the stone. It was the same in every quest, he thought. "We go to the end of the river, we'll find the Phoenix Gem," he promised.

They left the sun's light behind them.

Ian's staff shone in the dark and they could see amazing things. There was a picture of a big wizard on one wall. But the river went on and on.

"If we sail on something, we'll get there faster," Barley thought. He was eating some cheese snacks. He looked at one, then at Ian, and they both smiled.

"Magnora Gantuan!" Ian cried. Soon, they were sailing on the water on top of a very big cheese snack. This was better!

As they went deeper into the mountain Ian practiced his spells and talked to Barley about Dad.

Barley remembered something sad. When his dad was ill, Barley refused to see him. He was too scared. He always felt bad because he never said goodbye.

Laurel was driving fast when suddenly a Pixie Duster hit the glass in front of her. *SPLAT!* Laurel turned the wheel hard and the car went off the road.

She and the Manticore looked at the broken car. How could they get to the boys now?

Laurel watched the Pixie Dusters fly up into the air. Then she looked at the Manticore. "Have you ever thought about exercising those wings?" she asked, curiously.

Finally, the river ended, and Ian, Barley, and Dad walked along another path. Suddenly, a hole in the roof opened and something horrible and green dropped down.

The clothes on top of Dad's legs fell off. They disappeared inside the green thing!

Barley and Ian ran, pulling Dad behind them. Sharp sticks flew at them from the walls. They ran faster. There were dangers everywhere, just like in Barley's games! Then they came to a metal gate that was closing quickly. They got under it and found themselves in a room. In the middle of the floor, there was a round stone with a star on it.

"Don't step on that!" Barley said.

Suddenly, water started to fill the room. It came up to their necks and pushed them up to the roof. There was another stone with a star above them.

"Maybe I was wrong," Barley thought. "Maybe we needed to step on the stone." But they couldn't now. The water was too deep for Ian and Barley.

But Dad didn't need to breathe! The boys pushed Dad's legs down to stand on the stone in the floor. The roof opened!

There was a ladder. They climbed it, and Ian pushed up another round stone. Was this finally the end of their quest?

8 The Curse Rises

"This is crazy," Ian thought. They were on the road outside their school. He was angry. The Path of Peril was wrong. Why did he listen to his brother?

"We can still find the Phoenix Gem," Barley cried, but Ian led Dad off. The sun was low. Dad's day was nearly gone.

Ian looked sadly at his notes. He could never do these things with Dad now. Then he looked again. "Learn to drive". He remembered how Barley helped him on the expressway. He remembered the dancing, the laughing ...

"I've done all these things," Ian thought. "But not with Dad—with Barley." He smiled.

Barley looked at the fountain outside the school. It was old, from the days of magic. Could the end of their quest be there?

He climbed in and saw a hole that was the same shape as the stone. A secret space opened, and a bright orange light shone out. It was the Phoenix Gem!

He held it high to show Ian. "Yeah!"" he shouted.

"Behind you!" Ian cried. Red smoke was coming from the fountain. It filled the air and red fingers pushed in through the school doors and windows. Furniture, stones, and pieces of wall rose into the sky.

The fingers became a big dragon.

Barley ran.

Suddenly, the dragon fell. The Manticore was attacking it with the Curse Crusher and Laurel was riding on her back. The fierce animal turned and hit the Manticore with its heavy wing. She and Laurel fell to the ground.

Laurel picked up the sword and jumped on the dragon. "I can do this," she thought. "I am a fighter!" She pushed the sword into the dragon's red heart, but the animal was strong. It tried to push Laurel off.

Barley put the Phoenix Gem in the staff and Ian shouted the spell. Blue light shone brightly around Dad's legs.

The staff now shone red. The wind pushed Ian back, but Barley
helped him. Then, the Phoenix Gem rose into the air and stopped
above Dad's legs. Magic rained down.

   The dragon finally threw Laurel off its back. "Boys!" she cried.
   Barley turned to help her.

   "No!" Ian said. "You go and say goodbye. I never had a dad …
but I always had you." Ian ran to the dragon, shouting spells. The
staff shot blue light and knocked the animal on its back.

   Then Ian screamed "Accelior!" The sword rose from Mom's
hands and flew through the air. The Curse Crusher went deep into
the dragon's red heart.

Slowly the dragon broke into pieces and the curse was gone.

Ian suddenly felt weak and everything went black. When he woke, there were stones and bits of broken furniture all around him. A warm light was shining through the spaces.

Ian watched Dad and Barley talking. Then the sun dropped into the sea. Dad hugged Barley and his shape disappeared in hundreds of little gold stars.

"He said he's very proud of the person you grew up to be," Barley told Ian later. "Oh, and he told me to give you this," then he gave his little brother a big hug.

9 The Magic Has Returned

"Long ago, the world was adventurous, exciting, and full of magic!" Ian tells his class. "With a little bit of magic in your life ... you can do almost anything."

And there is magic at the Manticore's Tavern now. Corey talks about her dangerous adventures. She even breathes fire!

Ian has new friends, and Barley has a new van. "Best way to the park is to take the Road of Ruin!" he says.

"Mmm ..." The new, confident, Ian smiles. "On a quest, the clear path is never the right one!" Blue light shines all around Guinevere the Second, and they rise up into the air.

Magic is back to stay!

After You Read

1 **Who said these things? Why did they say them?**

> Barley   Ian   Laurel   Corey   The Pixie Dusters   Colt

1 "I have something for you."

2 "Look at that Manticore!"

3 "What have I become?"

4 "You're dead!"

5 "Just do one thing my way."

6 "You guys are in big trouble."

2 **Answer the questions.**

1 Why does Dad leave a gift for Ian and Barley?

2 Why does Dad only have legs?

3 How do the boys travel on their quest?

4 Why do the boys take the Path of Peril?

5 Why do the boys decide to follow the stone birds?

6 Why does Ian tell Barley to stay with Dad?

3 **Discuss with a friend.**

1 How has the Manticore changed in her life? Why?

2 Is it important to have adventure in our lives? Why?

3 What other spells do you think are in Ian's spell book?

4 What do you think is the main message of the story?

Glossary

confident (*adj.*) sure that you can do things well, talk easily to people, and try new things

curious (*adj.*) wanting to know about something

curse (*noun*) words that bring bad luck

disguise past tense **disguised** (*verb*) to change how you look so that people don't know you; *Ian disguised himself as Officer Colt Bronco, Mom's new boyfriend.*

dragon (*noun*) a big, imaginary animal that has wings, a long tail, and can breathe fire

expressway (*noun*) a wide road for fast traffic

fantasy (*noun*) a story, game, movie, etc., which comes from our imagination, and not facts

fountain (*noun*) something like a statue. Water rises through it and it is pretty to look at

gas (*noun*) something you put into a car so that it will drive

hug past tense **hugged** (*verb*) to put your arms around someone; *Barley hugged him. "You hear that, Dad? We're going on a quest!"*

like (*prep.*) nearly the same as something

magic (*noun*) a power that makes strange or impossible things happen

quest (*noun*) a journey to find something. It is often dangerous and takes a long time

rope (*noun*) something that is strong, thick, and made of many long strings

shake past tense **shook** (*verb*) to move from side to side; *Suddenly, the Phoenix Gem started to shine, and the staff began to shake.*

spell (*noun*) words that make magic things happen

staff (*noun*) a thick stick. People can use this to help them walk

sword (*noun*) a long, thin, sharp piece of metal used for fighting

tap past tense **tapped** (*verb*) to touch something lightly many times; *Barley tapped his fingers on one of the shoes.*

wizard (*noun*) a boy or man who can do magic

Play: The Past Is Important

Scene 1:

At Laurel's house. Officer Colt, Laurel's boyfriend, gets a phone call.

COLT: [finishing his call and speaking to Barley] Barley, Barley. Every time the city tries to pull down an old building, I gotta come out and help you.

BARLEY: [seeming not to understand] What are you talking about?

COLT: Listen to this.

[He plays a recording on his phone. We hear Barley's voice shouting:]

"I will not let you destroy this fountain. People have drunk from it for many centuries!"

LAUREL: Barley!

BARLEY: They're destroying the town's past!

Scene 2:

In the town. Barley has climbed into the fountain, looking for the Phoenix Gem. Some workers are there to pull down the fountain. One speaks to Barley. He knows him from the last time.

WORKER: All right, come on, out of the fountain.

BARLEY: [worried] I'm looking for something from the past. It's very old.

WORKER: Yeah, we know—the old days. [He pulls Barley away from the fountain.]

BARLEY: Stop! Please! Ow! Okay, I'm leaving!

Suddenly, Barley escapes from the workers and runs back to the fountain.

WORKER: Hey! Oh, come on. [Trying to pull Barley away. Barley holds on.]

Can someone call the police? We've got the crazy history guy again.

BARLEY: History is important!

Global Citizenship

Don't Pull it Down, Restore it!

Like Barley, the Young Person International Training Project knows that history is important. We can learn a lot from old buildings. We can learn what was important to the people then, how they lived, and how they built their towns and villages.

The Young Person International Training Project brings young people from all over the world together to learn about restoring old buildings. Isn't it amazing that people from different countries can work together? For example, young people from Taiwan can help students in Bulgaria to restore old buildings in their country.

As young people learn these new skills, they also learn about different cultures. Together, they find new ways to keep the past alive.

April 18 is the UNESCO World Heritage Day for Monuments and Sites.

Can people really do magic?

Magicians can make things appear and disappear, and change. Is this magic? No, it isn't. Magicians are clever people who use science to do things that seem impossible.

Mirrors Sometimes we think that something has disappeared, but really, we're looking at a mirror. If we put mirrors at special angles, they reflect light in different ways. Our eyes tell us something that isn't true. Look at this trick. With the mirrors, the magician makes us think there is only a head and no body!

Special mirrors can make us look different. If we look in a concave mirror, we are short and wide! In a convex mirror we're tall and thin!

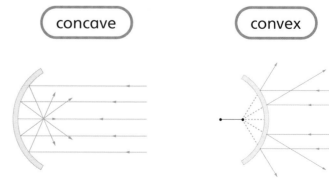

concave   convex

Harry Houdini (1874–1926)

Harry Houdini is perhaps one of the most famous magicians ever. He escaped from locked boxes, from under water, and he made an elephant disappear! Today, we know that he used small pieces of metal to open the locks, and secret doors in boxes. Mirrors and false walls hid the elephant. His magic worked because he, like many other great magicians, distracted the audiences at important times.

Today, magicians continue his work. Dynamo can walk on water. David Copperfield can make people rise in the air, like Ian's spell. We know that science can explain these things, but we still enjoy a little magic in our lives.

angle (*noun*) the space between two lines that meet
distract (*verb*) to make someone look away from something
magician (*noun*) a person who does magic
reflect (*verb*) to give back light, like a mirror or water does

Phonics

Say the sounds. Read the words.

ous

(dangerous)

(nervous)

ious

(curious)

(mysterious)

Read, then say the rhyme to a friend.

Ian was nervous and not very curious
About anything dangerous, different, or loud.
So, to be quite adventurous, in places mysterious
And become someone famous, it made him feel proud!